4799 2853

W9-BUW-042

WHAT IS
ST. PATRICK'S
DAY?

Elaine Landau

Enslow Elementary
an imprint of
Enslow Publishers, Inc.
40 Industrial Road
Box 398
Berkeley Heights, NJ 07922
USA
http://www.enslow.com

CONTENTS

WORDS TO KNOW

bagpipe—A musical instrument. It has pipes and a bag of air.

jig—A quick and lively Irish dance.

leprechauns (LEH pruh kahns)—Very little people from Irish tales. They are said to have magical powers. They are not real.

saint (SAYNT)—A very holy person. The Catholic church picks a saint after he or she dies. *Saint* can also be written as *St.*

shamrock (SHAM rock)—The shape of a clover leaf.

3

WHAT
HOLIDAY
IS THIS?

People wear green. They wear pins with silly sayings, like "Kiss me, I'm Irish." There are parades. It is St. Patrick's Day!

SAINT PATRICK'S

LIFE

St. Patrick was born more than 1,600 years ago. When he was young, he was a slave in Ireland. Later he told the Irish people about God. St. Patrick died when he was 75.

He was named Ireland's saint.

He watches over the people.

MOVING ON

Over the years, many Irish people came to the United States. They still loved St. Patrick. They honored his day here, too. People who were not Irish enjoyed the day with them. They still do.

PARADES
AND MORE

There are many parades on St. Patrick's Day. Bands play music. People wave Irish flags. Crowds watch and cheer. Sometimes the White House turns its fountain green!

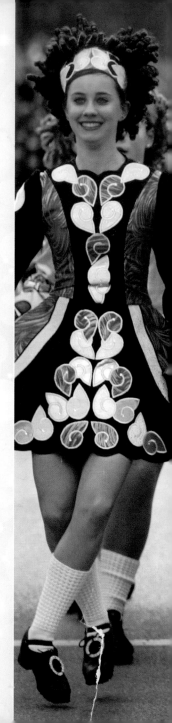

GOOD
EATING!

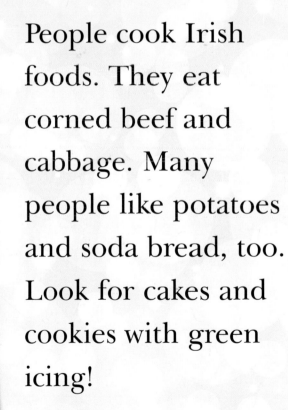

People cook Irish foods. They eat corned beef and cabbage. Many people like potatoes and soda bread, too. Look for cakes and cookies with green icing!

13

THERE ARE
PARTIES

People tell Irish stories.

They play Irish music.

People may play bagpipes.

They make a great sound.

Dance an Irish jig!

SYMBOLS OF
ST. PATRICK'S DAY

Green stands for Ireland's fields.

Shamrocks stand for good luck.

Leprechauns are little men in Irish stories.

They play tricks on people.

These things make people think of Ireland.

CELEBRATE EVERY YEAR

St. Patrick's Day is on March 17th. That is the day he died. You do not have to be Irish to love this day. On this day, everyone is Irish.

GROW
A CUP OF
GREEN!

Ireland has many fields of green grass. This year on St. Patrick's Day, you can grow some green grass of your own.

You Will Need:

❖ small package of oat seeds (You can find these at animal feed stores and some garden centers.)

❖ small plastic or paper cup

❖ potting soil

❖ water

What You Do:

Put about an inch of potting soil in the cup. Cover the top of the soil with oat seeds. Cover the seeds with a very thin layer of soil. Be sure not to put on too much soil. Add some water to wet the soil.

Place the cup in a sunny window. Water it a bit every day. In about five days, you will have your own cup of green grass. Happy St. Patrick's Day!

LEARN MORE

BOOKS

Berendes, Mary. *St. Patrick's Day Shamrocks*. Mankato, Minn.: The Child's World, 2010.

Gillis, Jennifer Blizin. *St. Patrick's Day*. Chicago: Heinemann Library, 2008.

Preszler, June. *St. Patrick's Day: Day of Irish Pride*. Mankato, Minn.: Capstone Press, 2007.

Rockwell, Anne. *St. Patrick's Day*. New York: HarperCollins, 2010.

WEB SITES

St. Patrick's Day Word Search

<http://www.kidsturncentral.com/games/wsearchstp. htm>

About St. Patrick's Day

<http://www.dltk-holidays.com/ patrick/about.htm>

INDEX

Enslow Elementary, an imprint of Enslow Publishers, Inc.
Enslow Elementary® is a registered trademark of Enslow Publishers, Inc.

Copyright © 2012 by Elaine Landau

Library of Congress Cataloging-in-Publication Data
    Landau, Elaine.
    What is St. Patrick's Day? / by Elaine Landau.
      p. cm. — (I like holidays!)
    Includes bibliographical references and index.
    Summary: "Provides information about how St. Patrick's Day is cele-
brated, popular symbols of the holiday, and a brief history. A St.
Patrick's Day activity is included"—Provided by publisher.
    ISBN 978-0-7660-3704-5
    1. Saint Patrick's Day—Juvenile literature. I. Title.
    GT4995.P3L37 2010
    394.262—dc22
                                2010006294

Paperback ISBN 978-1-59845-291-4

Printed in China

052011 Leo Paper Group, Heshan City, Guangdong, China

10 9 8 7 6 5 4 3 2 1

Photo Credits: © 1999 Artville, LLC, p. 9; Associated Press, p. 11; © The
Irish Image Collection/Photolibrary, p. 3 (saint), 7; © Peter Marshall/
Photolibrary, p. 4; © Richard Levine/Alamy, p. 19; © Robert Harding
Travel/Photolibrary, p. 8; Shutterstock.com, pp. 1, 2, 3 (bagpipe, jig,
leprechaun, shamrock), 12, 13, 15, 16, 17, 20, 23; White House Photo/
Lawrence Jackson, p. 10.

Cover Photo: Shutterstock.com

Series Consultant:
Duncan R. Jamieson, PhD
Professor of History
Ashland University
Ashland, OH

Series Literacy Consultant:
Allan A. De Fina, PhD
Dean, College of Education/Professor
    of Literacy Education
New Jersey City University
Past President of the New Jersey
    Reading Association